▶▶▶▶▶▶▶▶▶▶▶▶▶▶▶▶▶▶▶▶▶

Sister,

It's Not

Okay!

Library of Congress Catalog Card Number: 97-90957

ISBN 0-9660215-1-7

Printed in the USA by

MORRIS PUBLISHING

3212 East Highway 30 • Kearney, NE 68847 • 1-800-650-7888

For my daughter, Geisel,

and

For my sisters and their daughters:

Maxine

Marilyn & Shauun

Armelia, Angela, Sharon & Dottie

Juanita, Sandra, Cynthia, & Tracy

Janice, Nancy & Sharon

Ruby

Marie, Sheryl & Maresa.

Lovely ladies, all!

Many thanks to my husband,

Prince O. Teal, Jr.

and

to my friends,

Shirley Duhart Green

and Alce Delille

for their helpful suggestions

and

enthusiastic support of this project.

May God richly bless each of you, always!

Author's Autograph Page

For: _____

Inscription:

_____

_____

Author's Signature

Today's date: _____

This is a gift from: _____

Table of Contents

Sister, It's Not Okay!

Introduction

Chapter I	Having Babies out of Wedlock	8
Chapter II	Expecting Someone Else to Raise Your Child	11
Chapter III	Making Your Older Child Responsible for your Younger Child	17
Chapter IV	Talking Negatively to Your Child about His (or her) Absent Father	24
Chapter V	Supporting Your Child in a Wrong	30
Chapter VI	Keeping and Supporting a Man	38
Chapter VII	Letting a Man Spend the Night in Your Home in Your Bed (with your child's awareness)	45
Chapter VIII	Keeping Adult Children in Your Home and Supporting Them	51
Chapter IX	Raising Grandchildren While Your Own, Adult Children Party (live irresponsibly)	60
Chapter X	Making Welfare a Way of Life	72
Epilogue		82

Poem   **I Too Have A Dream**

Your Own Top Ten List

Sister, It's Not

Okay!

Introduction

Sister, there are a lot of things in this world over which we have absolutely no control: what the weather will be like tomorrow, if an expected child will be male or female, if our jobs will be phased out; will the company downsize? In fact, I could fill this page and probably a few others with events which are absolutely beyond our control and which are not okay even though we may be negatively impacted by them. But there are some things in our lives over which we are able to exert a good deal of control. In this book, I will discuss just ten of these things which are not okay. No doubt I could fill this page and quite a few others with events over which we do have a measure of control that are not okay, but I consider the following ten **The Top Ten.**

No doubt you can think of others which you would include in the top ten, but please consider the following **Top Ten** very seriously. Sister, it's not okay to:

(1) Have babies out of wedlock

(2) Raise your grandchildren while your own, adult children party (live irresponsibly)

(3) Keep able-bodied, adult children in your home, support and/or enable them

(4) Keep and support a man

(5) Support your child in a wrong

(6) Talk negatively to your child about his absent father

(7) Expect and/or allow someone else to raise your child

(8) Let a man to whom you are not married spend the night in your home in your bed (especially with your child's

awareness)

(9) Make your older child responsible for a younger brother

  and/or sister

(10)   Make welfare a way of life

Be woman enough to face the fact, Sister, that whether or not you've done one or more of the things on my top ten list, does not make it okay. Admit, if only to yourself, that it is wrong. Add your own list of **it's not okay** items to the one's listed above. Pledge to become a stronger woman, a better mother. Vow to practice only those behaviors that you want to see your children, or the children for whom you serve as role models, emulate. You'll be happier in the long run, and you'll raise happier children. You deserve to be happy. Your children deserve to be happy. They will not be happy if they cannot respect their mother. You have some control here. Exercise it! The control switch is in your hand!

Now, more about the **Top Ten:** Why, you might ask, should I not have a baby unless I'm married? Hopefully, your mother and grandmother taught you this; you know it's not okay. It's not scriptural, therefore, when it does occur, one should be discreet and humble because the situation is definitely inappropriate. You *do not* celebrate with a baby shower as if it is the same as expecting a baby within the sanctity of marriage. *It is not.* You don't celebrate immorality with a party, and when you do, you say not only to the world, for whom you may not be overly concerned, but to your other daughters and/or sisters as well, for whom it is expected that you will have a good deal of concern, that this is appropriate, *that this is okay,* when it very *definitely is not okay!*

"Why is it not okay for me to raise my grandchildren while my own adult children party, if that's what I want to do?" I hear someone ask. Simply put, because you end up resenting the fact that you are assuming the responsibility that your adult children should be assuming, and you find yourself resenting your adult children, consequently.

"What's wrong with keeping able-bodied, adult children in my home and supporting them?" you ask. What's wrong is your support and care enable your adult children to be lazy, irresponsible, and/or to take and hold jobs which do not require them to use their intelligence and/or skills acquired through the higher education which you have, in all probability, financed.

"Why can't I keep and support a man, if I want to do so?" you ask. Simply put, because by so doing, you lose, if you ever had, that man's respect, and more...

Why shouldn't I talk negatively to my child about his absent father? you are probably thinking. The mere fact that the father is absent is already one negative in your child's life. Don't add another negative by denigrating the child's father.

It's not okay to expect and/or allow someone else to raise your child. Having a child obligates you, and no one else, except the child's father, and that's only if you are married to him.

It's my bed; I'm paying for it. Why isn't it okay for me to let my man spend the night in it? It's my home; my child doesn't run it, I do. I'm the boss here. These will probably be someone's thoughts after reading these lines. Well, you're not running it very efficiently by setting the example which immoral behavior establishes. B.B. King sings about paying the cost to be the boss, and as the boss in your home, part of the cost exacted is setting a good example for your children. If you refuse to pay this cost, your children will be the losers.

"What's wrong with making an older child responsible for his or her younger brother or sister?" you ask. If it's so easy, you do it! If it's so hard, do you really think another child is up to the task?

Finally, to make welfare a way of life is to doom yourself and your children to a life of dependency. Do you really want to do that? Do you really want to limit what you can provide for yourself and your children just so you can continue to be supported by the government?

Please, consider the reasons given in this introduction, and find out even more about **The Top Ten** behaviors, Sister, that are really not okay. Upon honest reflection, I think you'll agree with me. Use the space made available in back of this book to add your own top ten behaviors in which we, as sisters, should not engage. Share them with another sister. As united sisters, we will triumph!

Lastly, having engaged in one, or even more than one, of **The Top Ten** behaviors which are not okay, does not mean that you are a bad person. But what it does, as a rule, is serve to make you an unhappy, unfulfilled, disrespected person. Aretha Franklin sings about a little respect. We, Sister, have sung the blues about being disrespected for generations. Yet, many of us have actively engaged in one or more of these Top Ten behaviors on an on-going basis, knowing that they are not right, giving no credence to how the behavior makes others feel about us and/or react to us. These behaviors foster disrespect!

Don't use past behaviors as justification for lowered self-esteem, or future inappropriate behaviors. Rise above the "Everybody's doing it" mentality. Make the decision that from this day forward some of these top ten behaviors may be a part of your history, but they will definitely not be a part of your future. You, and you alone, can and probably will, have the greatest impact upon how your child, or children, turn out in their adult lives. That's an awesome responsibility. Knowing what's not okay, and then making sure that you don't engage in the behavior sets a powerful example for your child. You, Sister, are at the controls. What will you activate by the switch you pull?

Sister, It's Not Okay

Chapter I

Having Babies out of Wedlock

Sister, plain and simple truth: **it is not okay to have a baby if you are not married.** The argument, "It's my body, and I can do whatever I want with it," won't wash. While it is your prerogative to use, and/or misuse your own body, I remind you that once the umbilical cord is severed, your baby is completely disconnected from your body. What then? Does he or she not have the right to an intact family? Does he or she not have the right to a loving, committed dad who will rejoice in his or her birth? Should what you want take precedence over what your child needs? These are questions to which every woman should give serious consideration before allowing herself to become pregnant by a man to whom she is not married.

We hear so much these days about men being unwilling to become involved in a committed relationship. Do you ever wonder why this seems to be so prevalent at all levels of society? I submit that the major reason why this is so is because a man these days doesn't have to commit to become a major player in a committed relationship. You, Sister, are willing to do all of the committing, failing to recognize, or to give credence to the recognition of the fact that the man has given no actual signs of being willing to commit. He can move into a house with you; he can share not only your home, but your bed, your body. He can drive your car, even when you know, and he knows, that your insurance coverage will not pay for any damage he sustains. You will even have his child when you know that he has no intention of committing, even when he has told you that he does not want a child. Don't pretend! "To thine own self be true," is a phrase with which you are well familiar. You learned a long time ago that a person who can get milk from a store has no need for a cow, or why buy the cow when you can get the milk free?

Now, think about it seriously. Can you come up with one good reason why a man who can have all of this, and his freedom too, will be motivated to relinquish his freedom? I don't think so. I know I can't!

Admittedly, time has wrought many positive changes, but one change wrought by time which is definitely not a positive one is the widespread practice of having babies out of wedlock. In generations past, this practice was not an accepted one, and it is still a practice which is frowned upon by people of God. Having a baby should be a family affair, and while we might not all agree that, "It takes a village to raise a child," we all do agree that it takes two people to make a baby. That being the case, every child ought to be welcomed into this world by at least two families, if not a whole village.

Young Sisters, those of you who have not yet begun your families, a baby is a gift from God, but it is a gift that He allows you to choose the conditions under which you receive. It is a gift created inside of your own body. Don't violate this precious gift by choosing to receive it illegitimately. Don't violate yourself! Sister, this is one situation over which you have total control. It is yours to command. What will you do? How will your precious baby begin life? You are the determiner!

Chapter II

Expecting Someone Else to Raise Your Child

Plain and simple truth, Sister: **it's not okay to expect nor to allow someone else to raise your child.** When you have a child, you instantly acquire the responsibility for his or her care, upkeep and raising. Your mother, your sister, your best friend, etc., are not obligated merely because you gave birth, but you are. You are largely responsible for how another human being turns out in life. That's a daunting undertaking! Don't undertake it lightly. Give serious consideration to whether or not it's one for which you are ready because once you have had a child, you are responsible for that child, and no matter who else assumes the responsibility for your child's care, that does not negate your responsibility.

When a child is being raised by any woman other than his or her mother, that person is acting as a surrogate. If the child's mother is alive and well, as a general rule, that child will come to resent the fact that it isn't his or her mother who is doing the parenting. For many children, and there are thousands within the public schools of this country who fall into this category, this causes them to "act out" their resentment in numerous ways. Some children who are being raised by surrogates give adult authority a hard time to get back at their mothers, whom they cannot give a hard time . Some of them become perfectionists, hoping that if they do everything "right," their "real" mothers will admire them and want them.   Others become chronic troublemakers at school, hoping this will get their mothers' attention, or that it will cause the surrogate to "give them back" to their "real" mothers. These children cannot, are not yet equipped, to handle the truth of the matter, which in most instances is: **if their "real" mothers wanted to raise them, they would probably already be in the process of so doing.** Some children are never able to face this reality, not even after they reach adulthood, and thus, they are crippled for life. You see, a fully functional human being must be willing to accept and admit the truth, even if he or she does so only to him or herself.

Make no mistake about it, Sister. Children want their mothers, plain and simple. This is the way it is supposed to be; this is the way it is! I believe God designed it this way, and when this is not the way it is, be assured that something is wrong with the picture. For a child to prefer someone else to his or her mother means that something has gone awry: has the mother left her child in the care of others for so long that the mother is a virtual stranger to the child? Is Mother abusing the child? Has Mother been ruled unfit? Is Mother unfit, though there has been no ruling? Does Mother neglect the child when he or she is in Mother's care? Does Mother show, consciously or subconsciously, that the child is keeping her from "doing what she really wants to do?"

And here I want to clarify something. If you have legally adopted a baby, you are that baby's mother. I recognize that as a fact; the law recognizes that fact. Although you are not the birth mother, you are the mother. I'm talking here about children who are being raised by grandmothers, mothers' friends, mothers' aunts, etc. I am not talking about legally adopted children who are being raised by the mothers who have legally adopted them.

Mothers who adopt children do so, almost always, because they want and are ready to be mothers.

Children are not stupid. The vast majority of them are intelligent as well as intuitive. They know when their mothers enjoy having them around. They know when they're wanted, even when it hasn't been articulated. All things being equal, rest assured a child prefers his or her mother.

With this in mind, know this: being tired after you've worked all day does not validate your feelings that someone else should chauffeur your child to and from after-school activities, that someone else should attend P.T.A. Meetings at your child's school, but not you, that someone else should get up at night to check on your child, that someone else should leave work early or unexpectedly to pick up your child when he or she gets sick at school, that someone else should take your child to medical appointments, that someone else should attend parent conferences, (and the list goes on). These are parental responsibilities, and even though there are times when they can be designated to be performed by someone else, they belong to you. Fix that thought firmly within your psyche. It's one that deserves serious reflection. If these are responsibilities which you rarely or never assume, ask yourself if these could be the reasons why your child is not doing well in school. Ask yourself if these are some of the reasons why your child, who was once so well behaved that his or her teachers complimented you for such a well-behaved child, is having constant referrals written on him or her now, or why your child needs an attitude adjustment now.

Believe it or not, your child notices if he or she is always the one who has to "bum" a ride. Children also notice if their moms are the ones from whom rides are always being "bummed." These kinds of things impact children. They tend to give a child a sense of belonging, a sense of being wanted, of being cherished; valued. Or they tend to give a child a sense of being a bother, of being "in the way," of being a nuisance. It is within your power to determine which of these feelings are internalized by your child. And it is incumbent upon you to understand that your child will internalize these negative or positive feelings, long before he or she is mature enough to articulate them.

Assume responsibility for the care of your child. Do so lovingly, and with a sense of humor. Certainly, at times these obligations can and will be burdensome, but that doesn't justify your neglect of them. Be cognizant of the fact that you can't neglect these responsibilities without neglecting your child. And children, just like the rest of us, resent being neglected.

As stated previously, the vast majority of children are intelligent. I know this for a certainty, having been a teacher in the public schools in excess of twenty years. So children know that certain things should be done for them by their own parents, and they want their own parents to do these things.

They are able to observe the positive interactions between other children and their parents, and they desire to participate in these same kinds of shared experiences with their own parents. Sure, Joe's dad can drop your son off for practice every day; he can pick your son up every day when he picks Joe up. But Joe's dad is Joe's dad, not your son's dad. And your son does know the difference. He is able to see as well as feel the difference.

Sister, if you don't already know, I want to share this truth with you: your child is the beneficiary when you are in possession of the kind of knowledge that can make a positive difference in how your child feels about him or herself.

Chapter III

Making Your Older Child Responsible for Your Younger Child

Sister, plain and simple, **it is wrong for you to make your older child responsible for your younger one.** When you have children, ideally you and your husband, the children's father, are the responsible parties. Of course, no one needs to tell you that we do not live in an ideal world. This being the case, you are likely to be responsible, all by yourself, Sister, for raising your children. It is natural to want and to need help with this monumental, though rewarding task, but please, do not make your older child share the burden of parenting your younger one.

Why? You may ask. I helped with my younger brothers and sisters, you are probably thinking. But I submit that helping with younger siblings is not the same as having it drilled into you that you are responsible for a child. It is not the same as being punished when "Mama" gets home because of what your younger sibling did, or did not do. It is not the same as being told that you can't participate in any after-school activities because you must rush home to care for a younger brother or sister. It is not the same as having been brainwashed into thinking that once you get yourself through college, you are obligated to pay for the education of a younger brother or sister.

Now please do not misinterpret this. There are many large families in which older siblings have chosen to assume the responsibility for paying the tuition for a younger sibling. But the operative word here is **chosen.** If, out of devotion, respect, and a feeling of being loved and nurtured, one sibling chooses to bear the expenses for tuition costs of another, this is admirable. It should, however, definitely be that older sibling's choice. That older sibling should not be made to feel guilty because he or she wants to get married, or wants to move to a distant city, or wants to make some other choices. That should be his or her prerogative as an adult human being, and it should be instilled that he or she is responsible only for him or herself, until such time as he or she brings a child into this world, at which time he or she then becomes responsible for that child.

Let's face it: being responsible for a child is a heavy responsibility, even for fully mature adults. But to lay something this heavy on your child is to rob your child of his or her childhood. Your child is not accountable, nor should be made to feel accountable, for his brother or sister. Face that fact, and deal with it. If you don't, your child will resent you, and rightfully so, for making him or her feel responsible at a time in his or her life when he or she should be free of parental responsibility. It may take years for this resentment to surface, but it will eventually surface. You see, it is natural for a child to desire to be looked upon favorably by a parent. Consequently, most children will do whatever it takes to please a beloved parent, and this includes assuming responsibility for a younger sibling. The older child may even enjoy this responsibility initially, but we all know that the novelty wears off all too soon. And as each of us can attest, childhood being a temporary state, as your older child begins to mature, he or she also begins to realize the many times when a pleasure, some privilege or request was denied, which should, and probably would have been granted, if responsibility for a younger sibling had been no factor. Then, resentment begins to set in.

Consider the following real occurrence in the life of a friend of mine who is now deceased. I'll give her and her sister and brother fictitious names here. Patrice, my friend, is four years older than Al, her brother, and almost six years older than her sister, Pat. When I met Patrice, their dad was in prison. The two of us were young adults at the time. We had both recently graduated from college; we were both newlyweds, and were beginning our careers in education.

From the first, Patrice declared that she wanted no kids. Period! Ever! On the other hand, I couldn't wait to have a baby. I couldn't even remember a time that I didn't look forward to getting married and having a baby.

As time passed and we got to know one another really well, she shared with me that as the eldest of three children, she was responsible for her younger brother and sister while their mother worked (remember, her dad was in prison, so her mother was raising them alone). Her brother was relatively easy, she said. As long as he was full, he mostly amused himself or played with friends in the neighborhood.

Her sister, Pat, was a whole, different story. She constantly threw temper tantrums, threw things, ignored Patrice's directions and/or requests, etc. Pat behaved the same way with their mother, but their mother punished Patrice because their mother said, "If you didn't let her get away with that stuff while I'm at work, she wouldn't try it when I'm at home!"

This continued for a number of years. Patrice confessed to actually feeling responsible for Pat. She worked so hard at getting Pat to be obedient and cooperative, and there was some gradual improvement, she said. But it wasn't until Pat began first grade, at which time Patrice was almost twelve years old, that it was learned that Pat was deaf. Pat had been totally deaf since birth, and a lot of her tantrums and other behaviors had been dictated by her deafness. During the years when Patrice had had to care for Pat, she made the decision that she never wanted children. She remembered all the time she'd spent trying to potty train a totally deaf child, all of the punishments and spankings she got because Pat continued to soil herself long after the time their mother believed she should have already been potty trained, all of the after-school activities in which she could not participate because she had to rush home to be there for her brother and sister. She insisted that she'd had enough of that to last her a lifetime, that she wanted no part of it, ever again. Even though her brother, in later years, graduated from college, and her sister attended and graduated from a school which educates deaf children, having to be responsible for her brother and sister when she, herself, was a mere child, left its mark, indelibly, on Patrice.

You can see, I hope, or at the very least imagine, how Patrice must have felt. She had to potty-train her sister, who couldn't hear. She had to teach her sister to use a spoon and a fork; it was her job to teach Pat to look both ways before crossing the street. These, and countless others, are all behaviors for which a mature, adult parent, should assume responsibility for the teaching of. But from age seven through twelve or thirteen, Patrice was responsible for doing all of these things. At age six or seven, she was little more than a baby herself, but she had been assigned the adult responsibility of raising a two-year old sibling. And she took this responsibility seriously. And who knows, if Pat had been cared for daily by a responsible adult, maybe her deafness would have been recognized years earlier.

Patrice also shared with me that having this responsibility so early in life made her into a serious person, and also a bossy one. Looking back upon it, she believed the major reason why her marriage failed was because she was dictatorial and bossy. Little wonder, when you think about the fact that she became a surrogate parent at such an early age. So it's easy to see how Patrice was impacted, for life, by having to "raise" younger siblings.

Sister, allow your children, all of them, to enjoy childhood. It will encourage them to joyfully anticipate the time when they too, are responsible adults and can begin their own families. Childhood, at best, is temporary. Soon enough children become adults and will have their own families, for whom they will be truly responsible, and part of your culpability to them is to teach them, by the example you set, that they are responsible for raising their own children.

Chapter IV

Talking Negatively to Your Child about His Absent Father

Sister, another plain and simple truth: **it is not okay to talk negatively to your child about his or her absent father.** No matter how much you may despise the man, no matter how justified you may be in feeling the way you do about him, no matter how despicable he may be, in your opinion, he is still your child's father, and it is a matter of record that children who feel good about their parents, tend to feel good about themselves. If your child's father is a truly despicable human being, make no mistake about it, your child will make this observation and come to this conclusion with no help at all from you. And this is as it should be. You see, a child has a right to love, and to be loved by, both of his parents, and ideally, to be raised by them both. But while we must acknowledge that most of us are not privileged to live under ideal circumstances, we must likewise acknowledge that we are responsible for creating conditions that are as close to ideal as possible for our children. We can't do that by drilling into our sons and daughters that their fathers are monsters.

Many of our children misbehave at school, and when confronted with this misbehavior, have been heard to remark, "I'm just like my dad." Sister, don't give your son or daughter a ready-made excuse for misbehavior; for failure. Remarks like, "You're a sorry bum, just like your father; you look just like him; you act just like him too, and I can't stand either one of you! You're a stupid so and so, just like your dad!" serve not only to make your children feel negative about their father, but also about themselves, and about you too. These kinds of remarks are not pleasant to a child's ears. Remarks like these cause your child to resent you. These kinds of remarks lessen your child's willingness to strive for excellence. They provide your child with what he or she considers valid reasons for why he or she can't understand math, or doesn't like science, or can't sit still, or can't behave appropriately, etc.

Your child will probably never tell you that this is so. Children usually do not understand how profoundly they have been impacted by these kinds of negative remarks about their fathers, and even when they do come to understand, it is a rare child who will tell Mother that her remarks have negatively impacted him or her. This is one reason why you need to hear it from someone else, and take it to heart.

The fact that you are no longer married to the child's father, or never were married to him, does not alter the fact that the man who fathered your child is your child's father. Bear in mind that it doesn't take a child very long these days to learn about the sexual activity that had to take place to produce him or her. Bear in mind that your child knows, without quite understanding how he knows, that the responsibility for choosing his father was, in all likelihood, your decision. What do you think this says to your child about you that you would select this "monster" to father him? You are not blameless in the matter. Face this reality: more than likely, you willingly participated in your child's conception.

I do not suggest that you make excuses to your child for the sake of creating a false image of the father in his or her mind. But you do not necessarily do this if you do not caluminate the child's father. For a brief period, the child will probably operate under the illusion that the father is the "good guy," and that you are the "bad guy." This is so because you are the one who is there to insist upon rules being followed, chores being done, homework being completed, etc. Be the mature adult in this matter; realize that if this is an illusion, it is one of temporary duration. At this point, don't try to be your child's friend. It's not friendship that your child needs from you, it's parenting! This is doubly true if his father is not in the picture. This effort on the part of many parents to appear to be the "good guy," and to be their child's pal, frequently backfires. Your child needs someone who parents him, who guides him, who makes him understand that there is a right way and a wrong way, and that a mother's love impels her to direct her child down the right path. When the father is not in the picture, a mother has to perform double duty. Many women are aware of this, and do an admirable job of it. Is it fair? Of course it isn't fair, but one of the lessons that we're responsible for teaching our children is that life is not always fair.

Finally, do not resent your child because he or she bears a physical resemblance to his or her father. What part did the child play in bringing about this reality? Once again, you are not blameless in this matter, but your child is totally blameless. Why should you make your child suffer because he or she looks like the man you chose to father him or her? You were totally aware, before the fact, that the child gets his or her physical attributes from Mom and Dad. So you knew at the outset that your child may, or may not, resemble the father. Don't force your child to pay for a deed in which he or she had no hand!

Do the Godly thing: pray for the grace to get beyond your negative feelings about your child's father. Embrace and love your child for himself, not as an extension of you, or anyone else. Make it clear to your child, by your behavior if not by the words you use, that you love him for himself, not because he resembles you, or your mother, or someone else upon whom you look favorably. Make it clear to your child that you love him, in spite of the fact that he resembles someone upon whom you do not look favorably. Be aware that your child knows that you don't look favorably upon his father, if this is indeed the case, even when you don't denigrate his father. Again, children are intelligent, and they begin to understand, very early in their lives, when their parents don't really like one another. Don't force him to feel rejection from you as well as from his absent father.

When you embrace and love your child for himself, you'll feel a peace that you have not previously known, a peace which comes from facing the reality that you bear part of the blame, that your child is blameless, and that if a penalty is to be paid, it is not your child who owes the debt!

Chapter V

Supporting Your Child in a Wrong

Sister, one of the worst injustices you can foster upon your child is to support your child when he or she has done wrong. This does not mean that you withdraw your love and/or understanding from your child. I would never suggest or encourage that. But what it does mean is that you let your child know, using no uncertain terms, that he or she is wrong, that you don't like it, and that you won't tolerate a recurrence of the behavior. Let your child know that you won't hide the behavior to protect him, that the best way to keep a behavior from being exposed is not to engage in it!

Consider the following scenario: John, a thirteen year old boy in eighth grade, is dropped off at school almost daily by his father, as his father is on his way to work. Mary, John's mother, is totally aware that this is so.

At the end of the first grading period when John receives his first report card for the new school term, Mary notices that John was tardy on ten separate days for his first period class. She wonders why this was so, but she doesn't confront him about it. John's first period class is reading. John fails reading for the first grading period. His parents are summoned to the school for a conference.

When the conference is held, all of John's core teachers are in attendance. They each talk briefly about John's behavior and academic progress in their classes. His reading teacher tells them, "John is late almost daily for my class. I teach him reading during the first period."

"But I drop him off at school every day on my way to work," John's dad, Mr. Johnson says. "Why would he be late for first period?" he asks.

"I have no idea why he's late, and I had no idea that you were dropping him off," the reading teacher says. "I had assumed that his lateness was due to the fact that he walked to school and probably didn't leave home early enough to make it to first period on time," she concludes. "John, why are you late so frequently if your dad is dropping you off at school?" she asks.

"He don't drop me off every day. Some days I do walk to school," John says. John's English teacher is about to correct his grammar error, but his mother cuts in.

"He does walk sometimes," his mother says quickly. As she says this, John's father is looking at John's report card. It is a duplicate which his teachers requested for the conference. John's mother did not show the copy that John brought home to his dad. She doesn't want any trouble between them.

Sister, know this: when you keep things about your son from his father, especially things concerning your son's inappropriate behavior, you are saying to your son, in effect, that you don't want him to have to answer to his dad for his misbehavior. You are telling him that he shouldn't have to pay for his misdeeds. You are saying to your son that you understand his misbehavior, but that his father won't understand it. At that very moment, your son may be receiving the message that any woman in his life who loves him will be understanding about his lies, whatever they are. This could be a message that could doom any future, adult relationship that he might have with a woman. You are saying that you, and consequently all women, are less demanding of appropriate behavior from him than his dad, or any man would be. These are not messages you should be sending to your son. These are not messages that help to foster a strong father/son relationship. These are not messages that help a boy to mature into a man who is willing to be accountable for his actions. Think about the messages that you pass on to your child. Make sure they are ones you want him to receive.

"But it says here that he was late ten times for first period; I just counted them. He might've walked once or twice. I'll even go as high as three or four times, but it's no where near ten times. What is this late business about, Boy?" Mr. Johnson says.

John does not respond, nor does he look at his dad. He keeps his eyes on the floor. He is the only one in the room who knows why he has been late for first period so many times, but he doesn't share that information with the group gathered there for the conference.

"I'm the cause of him being late some of those times," Mrs. Johnson says. Mr. Johnson gives her a suspicious glance, as if he is used to her making excuses for John, but he says nothing.

Sister, you are doing John a grave injustice. John is still a child. One of your obligations to him is to teach him to admit when he is wrong. If you don't teach him that he must assume responsibility for his own actions, who else is going to do so? I hear sisters complain quite frequently about irresponsible men who won't assume responsibility for their actions. Well, don't forget that most of these men were raised by their own mothers whose job it was to teach this behavior. Now you have the chance to raise a responsible boy so that he becomes a responsible man. Please Sister, don't support your child in a wrong. **It sends the wrong messages to him. It sends: maybe this wasn't as bad as I thought. It sends, I can get away with lying; I can easily lie my way out of trouble; she'll believe anything I tell her, maybe other people are as easily fooled.** And who knows what else children think when they know they are wrong, but that their own mothers are willing to justify them? And make no mistake about it: children do know when they are wrong!

Sister, it is not okay to support your child in a wrong, plain and simple truth. Don't do it. You don't help, you hurt your child, and no matter how well-intentioned you are, you need to be aware that to do so can cause irreparable damage. It can begin to establish character flaws in your child that he or she may never be rid of, the same kind of character flaws that we have recognized in some men who lie without batting an eye, and who will even lie to their children, making promises to them that they have no intention of keeping. Please, Sister, don't do that to your child!

You know, Sister, that your child is intelligent enough to know when he is wrong. What message do you think you send when you lie for him? How do you interpret that message? Do you interpret that message? **Consider this: our children often test us, and if we're found wanting, they often use this to justify their own misbehavior.** Is this what you want for your child?

Sister, you are obligated, like it or not, to set a good example for your child. You fail to do so when you lie to justify your child's inappropriate behavior. You do not gain or maintain your child's respect by lying for him. He knows that it is wrong to lie, but if Mom does it, maybe it's not as wrong as he thought, he could decide. Don't do that to your child. Like your child, you already know right from wrong. Choose the right; you won't regret it!

Know this: "We see the world not as it is, but as we are." If you want your child to see the world in a way that fosters uprightness, honesty, integrity, and all of the qualities possessed by those whom we admire most, you must assist him to develop these qualities. If you do this, when he sees the world as he is, he will also see it as it ought to be, as God means him to see it: as a functional human being who has not become dysfunctional, in part, because his mother has supported him when he was wrong and has, consequently, assisted him in developing this dysfunctionalism.

If you don't support your child in "little" wrongs, your child will never approach you seeking your support in "big" wrongs. Consider the young man who asks his mother if he can hide stolen goods in her basement, or the boy who asks his mother if he can put a stolen bicycle in the garage. Don't let it reach such a point. Head it off at the entrance! When your child is wrong, don't support him in it, or try to cover for him. Make it clear that you disapprove of his behavior, and not of him. Make your child understand clearly that you expect him to admit when he is wrong. When you do this, your child will be far less likely to repeat the behavior.

One other thing requires mentioning in this chapter. Sisters, whether you are aware of this or not, it needs to be pointed out that those of us who work with children hear far more excuses from mothers for their sons than we do for their daughters. Perhaps Sisters, we feel more guilty about our sons being without their fathers as role models in their lives than we do about our daughters being without fathers, and we attempt to "Make it up to our boys," by making excuses for them. Whatever the reasons, this is an observed fact by those of us who work with children on a regular basis, and it is one that needs to be examined closely, and eliminated. As long as we attempt to excuse our boys' inappropriate behaviors, we will be sending our sons messages which they should not be receiving, messages which could possibly condemn any future, long-term relationships they may seek to establish with women when they, themselves, have become men. That is not what we want! Is it?

Chapter VI

Keeping and Supporting a Man

Sister, if the price of having a man in your life is keeping and supporting him, then the price is exorbitant. **It is not okay to keep and support a man.** There are a number of reasons why this price is too high. First and foremost, men don't respect women who keep and support them, and Sister, you don't need any man in your life who does not respect you. Another reason why this price is too high is because it sets an example that you do not want to set for your son and/or daughter.

Girls who see their mothers keep and support a man lose respect for their mothers, but at the same time, they are twice as likely to repeat this behavior when they reach adulthood as are girls who have not observed this behavior in their mothers. Why? Because it is a pattern to which they are accustomed, or at the very least, one with which they are familiar. It is a pattern that sets a poor example for your daughter. It gives her the message that in order to get a man, you must be willing to support him. It gives a message that you are not of value, so no man wants you for yourself, but for what you are willing to provide for him. These are messages that you do not want to give to your daughter. You want the messages she receives from you to be ones that promote a healthy self-image!

Another important deterrent to keeping and supporting a man is that he is, and can be, alone with your daughter while you are away from the home at work. This is not a pattern you want to establish in your home. Our daughters are precious to us and are deserving of our protection. We fail to protect them when we leave them at home, in bed alone, asleep and vulnerable, with a strange man in the home. Do not balk at the term, "strange." Rest assured this man will seem strange to your daughter if he approaches her bed as she lays sleeping. Rest assured that you set the stage for just such a scenario when you keep and support a man, if you have children in your home.

Another important reason why it is not okay, Sister, to keep and support a man, is because your son will take many of his cues from what he observes in his home environment. We want better

for our sons. We want them to develop into the kinds of men that ·
we hope our daughters will one day meet and marry. We want
them to look with revulsion upon the idea of being a "kept man."
We don't want them to see being "kept" as something to be proud
of, something to brag about, something to desire and seek after.
We want a good deal of their motivation for wanting to be
successful in life to be so that they can take care of themselves
first, and then any future families which they may have. We are
obligated, and doubly so when the boys' fathers are not present in
the homes, to provide them with positive, male role models.
Sisters, we don't do that when we keep and support a man because
men who are positive male role models do not allow themselves to
be "kept" by women.

Sisters, so many of our boys come to school on a daily basis
with chips on their shoulders. Once upon a time, this was not so.
But once upon a time most of our boys were being reared in homes
with their biological mothers and fathers. Today, this is not so.
Most of our children, both male and female, are being reared in
single-parent households, the majority of which are headed by
single moms. As our children near or reach their adolescent years,
they are frequently left alone with no supervision when we, Sisters,
are at work. Our children are forced, consequently, to grow up.

Well, children don't grow up in just those areas which allow them to stay home alone and supervise themselves, they grow up in other areas too. Boys, therefore, begin to resent it when "some" man is closed up in his mother's room with her. They resent that this man has access to "Mother," and they, themselves, do not. They resent what they imagine takes place behind the closed door. And who knows where their imagination takes them. Keep in mind that these are adolescent and/or preadolescent children whose sexual knowledge is not extensive, probably limited to what they've seen on a screen, read in a book, or heard from other children whose knowledge on this topic is equally limited. So although no one knows exactly what is in a boy's mind when his mother is behind a locked door with this man, it does not require a long reach to understand that he begins to feel resentment. This resentment sets the stage for the chip on the shoulder.

These boys leave their homes each morning already emotionally upset because their mothers, many of whom didn't even peek out the bedroom door to say, "Be sure to eat your cereal; wear your coat today; let me see what you're wearing this morning," have neglected to do this. Many of these boys are late for school countless mornings, waiting around until the last possible minute to leave home, hoping their moms will peek out the door and at least say, "Have a good day," or ask if they have money for lunch, or show some sign that they are as important to their mothers as the men are with whom they have spent the night.

Don't you know that it doesn't take very long for resentment to set in when this kind of neglect is a daily occurrence in a child's life? And believe me, these are daily occurrences in the lives of plenty of our children.

Nevertheless, these are children, and so they are not very sure where to place the blame or who the target should be. Consequently, many of them become unguided missiles looking for a target. Naturally, the targets of the blame must be people in these children's environments with whom they have contact. For so many of our boys, it becomes their male teachers. These boys will do fine in their classes which are taught by females, but as soon as they get to their first class of the day which is taught by a male, they get into trouble and get kicked out. Perhaps in their minds, maybe even at the subconscious level, they are getting back at those "dudes" who denied them access to their mothers.

Because these boys love their mothers, they cannot put the blame where it belongs. You see, they are just boys and are not mature enough to face the reality that the control switch is in "Mother's" hand. Consequently they, of necessity, must place the blame elsewhere. By so doing, they cause themselves continuous problems; they cause problems in the school environment. Many of them end up in the criminal justice system at a very early age, good boys who just needed what every child needs, to be embraced and loved and supervised during their adolescent and preadolescent years, but were not.

We hear on television and radio, we read in newspapers, about all of the violence prevalent in today's society. We complain about dangers we face if we come out of a mall at night, muggings, drive-by shootings, pocketbook snatching, etc. Well, consider this: people who walk around with chips on their shoulders usually get them knocked off, and when these chips are invisible, they sometimes get knocked off inadvertently.

Sisters, I know you have needs and desires. But our children must be our first consideration. We cannot allow our efforts to fulfill our needs and desires take priority over the needs and desires of our children. We all recognize and admit that our children need our love, supervision, and attention. They need to be embraced by us. They need to know that they are our priority. This must not mean that we make them our God, but we must make it clear to them that they are the most important people in our lives. Our behaviors must dictate this to them; to do less is to fail our children and to set them up for failure. Our children desire our attention, our involvement in their lives. They desire the peaceful home lives that only we, their parents, are responsible for providing for them. They may also desire a lot of the material things they see and hear about through commercials, peers, etc. But none of these things has any lasting significance as the giving to them of ourselves does. We must not be the cause of the invisible chips on the shoulders of our sons, because though the chips may be invisible, the results of having them there are very, very visible: constant phone calls from teachers, poor grades, insolence, anger, disrespect, poor self-esteem. gang affiliations, involvement in the criminal justice system, etc. Ask yourself, Sister: "What role am I playing in all of this?" Are you the diffuser or the diffusee?

Chapter VII

Letting a Man Spend the Night in Your Home in Your Bed with Your Child's Knowledge

Plain and simple truth, Sister: **if you want to be respected by your child, you cannot invite a man to come into your home to share your bed, if he is not your husband.** It may take years before you find out that your child does not respect you, or it may take only minutes, hours or days, especially if your child is a teenager when this happens, but your child knows that this isn't right, especially if you are raising him or her in the church, and as soon as it becomes necessary for you to correct your child, or deny him or her something that he or she wants to do, the child will point out to you the error of your ways.

Consider this: You cannot teach your child to respect the home if the child perceives that you do not respect the home. Inasmuch as it is in the home where the child first learns about respect, it is of utmost importance that you, Sister, set the example of respect that your child can emulate. You bear the responsibility in this. Nothing in your life can take precedence over setting the right example for your child, and this includes your love life.

Hear this: Your child's love life takes precedence over yours! And your child loves you dearly. It is very difficult for your child to admit, even to himself (and here I'm using him to mean either and/or both male and female) that his mother sleeps with a man (or men) to whom she isn't married. Who knows what goes on in the mind of a child who feels that his mother is doing something wrong, but he has no power to stop it, and can't even acknowledge it to himself? There is pain involved in not being able to respect and love one's mother, so even though no one knows what the child's thoughts are, we do know that some of these thoughts cause discomfort. stress; pain. And this we also know, Sister: that a mother's choices impact her children. and that the impact will yield either positive or negative results. There will be fallout

and you, Sister, are largely the determiner of whether it's good or bad.

We've all heard the question, "What am I supposed to do, put my life on hold because I have a child?" The answer is a resounding "YES!" If, by "putting your life on hold," you mean give up those things which have the potential to impact your child in a negative way, that is precisely what you are supposed to do. Don't forget, you had a choice about whether or not to become a mother. Your child had no choice, and still has none in the matter of whether or not **you are** his mother! You will always be your child's mother, even if you negate your responsibilities to him, but your child will not always be your child. One day he will be an adult to whom you gave birth, and many of the choices which he makes will be based, in part, on the examples you set for him when he was a child.

You're as aware as I am that some people spend their whole lifetimes nearly, trying to find the mothers who abandoned them, even when they have never even seen or heard from these mothers, even when they have been raised by loving, even doting, surrogates. This says something to all of us about the strong influence merely giving birth has on the lives of the ones born to us. Dare we, Sister, allow something as trivial as our misguided notions of what it means to 'live our lives,' something as trivial as our needs and desires for sexual gratification, cause us to blatantly disrespect our children, and then later expect to be able to demand their respect; later to expect them to behave in a respectful manner? That's not logical, Sister!

We've all heard that once upon a time children were expected to, "Do as I say, not as I do," by their parents and the other adults in their world. Well, if those times ever did exist when children did as they were told, not as the adults in their lives did, we will all readily agree that they exist no more. These are times when children are doing exactly as they see us do, and more. These are times when we know that we can get their respect only if we have shown ourselves to be respectable, and even then we sometimes have to demand it. What chance do you think you have of being respected by your child if your child deems you to be unworthy of respect? The decision is yours, it is one of the things that is within your power to control. The consequences of the decision you make regarding this situation might not be!

Don't risk something as important as your child's future for the sake of having a man in your bed. If it has to be, it doesn't have to be in your bed in your home. Put the needs of your child above the needs of your body. Your child deserves the very best.

Be the very best mother that you can possibly be for your child. Maybe there are a lot of things that you cannot give to your child. But there is one thing that only you can give to him: **a respectable mother!**

Don't use the excuse of creating a father figure for your child (or children) to bring this man into your home, your bed. You know that this is probably just an illusion. A real man who desires to be a real father figure for your children will not set the negative example of spending the night in your home in your bed. He will be concerned about the impression this will make on the children.

While it is true that your child does need a father, it is not likely that a man who has no intention of committing to you will become committed to your child. But it is likely that your child will begin to bond with this man. Possibly, your child wants a real father as badly as you want one for him. But since this man is probably a passing mirage in your child's life, when he leaves, this creates just another loss for your child. Don't do that to him! Love him enough to protect him from additional pain of abandonment, the pain he has likely already experienced when his father left the home, or additional pain of rejection, the pain he possibly already feels because his father has never been in his life. Your child will have pain, because pain is a part of life, but his pain does not have to result from a choice his mother makes in this matter. If you love your child enough to make him or her your first priority, you will not cause him or her pain because of a foolish choice you make to let a man to whom you are not married share your bed in the home which you are providing for your child. This is one decision which is yours, and yours alone!

Chapter VIII

Keeping Adult Children in Your Home and Supporting Them

Simply put, Sister, **it is not okay to allow your adult children to live in your home while you support them or subsidize their support.** As you work hard to raise your own children, let them know that your prayer is that you (and their father, if he is in the home) will be the ones privileged to parent them and to raise them to adulthood. Make it clear to them that you consider it a privilege to have them, and to be the one who takes care of their needs. They need to know that they are a source of joy and pride to you. Teach them, lovingly, that one of the reasons why they must work hard to succeed in school is because they must prepare for the time when they will be expected to take care of themselves. Let them know that you would be remiss in your instructions to them if you did not raise them with the awareness that your desire and intention to provide for their needs are because they are children, your children, and that you have the expectation that they are preparing themselves, with your assistance, for the time when they will be able to, and desirous of providing for their own needs. Teach them, by example as well as verbal instructions, that responsible, able-bodied, adults take care of themselves, that that is the way they like it, and that it is also the way that it is supposed to be. Let them know that you have no intention of taking care of them for the rest of their lives, nor yours, that you have every intention of helping them to prepare themselves so that when they become adults, they will be productive, self-supporting citizens. Teach this lesson throughout your child's life so that it becomes a natural part of his (and his is used here to refer to both male and female), thought processes. Teach it in such a way that your child just naturally expects to succeed in school, go on to college or some other life training, to get a job or start a business, and to become independent. You do not need to, nor should you send the message, "I'll be glad to be rid of you." The message that you send, instead, should be, "I'm grateful that God gave me intelligent children with the ability to be successful and independent in life. I expect, and will accept, no less from you. To do so would be to fail you, and I love you too much to do that." Be aware that neither of these messages has to be verbalized, even though it certainly can't hurt to verbalize the latter. But one or the other will be internalized by your child based upon you and your child's mutual life interactions.

It will do no good, Sister, for you to complain about your adult children invading your space. Don't allow this scenario to develop in your life or theirs. While raising them, teach this lesson throughout their formative years. Never miss an opportunity to point out that hard work and success are Siamese twins, that they are joined. If you do this throughout your children's formative years, you'll have adult children who anticipate beginning their lives independent of their parents' support because they will know that it is expected of them; they will have come to expect it of themselves, and to desire it. It becomes a source of pride to your children to be able to care for themselves when they have been reared to expect to do so when they become adults. Teach them that good habits create winners, so that they begin, early in their lives, to form the good habit of working hard, with this awareness!

Just as your children were proud of themselves when they learned to tie their own shoes, to button their own coats, etc., because they understood that to do so were accomplishments, as they mature, they will feel pride in the accomplishment of their own independency. To become independent becomes a natural expectation when your children are taught these principles throughout childhood. They will know, without having to be told, (and telling them certainly won't hurt), that you are proud of their independence, that they have done what you expected them to do, and that in so doing, they have pleased themselves as well as their parents. They will be ready when they have their own children to perpetuate this fine example. That's how you build a lasting legacy of which you and your family can be proud!

In the words of our children, **"Don't even go there!"** Don't waste energy entertaining the thought that it means you don't love your children, or that you love them less, because you are raising them to desire independence when they become adults. What self-respecting adult doesn't want to be independent and able to support him or herself? You are doing your children an injustice if you don't begin to teach them, early in life, that it is a parent's job to support and care for a child, but that adults are expected to care for and support themselves. It will follow, naturally, that once this message has been internalized by children, they will have added incentive to succeed because of the expectation that, "I must prepare to take care of myself." You are obligated, Sister, to teach this lesson to your child. If you fail to do this, you will be failing your child! Always remember that good habits create winners, and with this in mind, you will realize that it is incumbent upon you to begin to assist your child to develop good work habits early in life.

Think about the constant complaints you hear, repeatedly, from people with whom you are acquainted about their adult offspring who still live at home:

1. He's lazy; he expects me to take care of him!

2. He lays up in here for most of the day, then complains when I get on him about it, saying that he can't find a job.

3. He says he just won't work for minimum wage; it's slave wages.

4. Every time I say something to her, she reminds me that she's a grown woman. Well, I wish she'd act like it and find herself somewhere else to live!

5. He's a college graduate, yet he won't even look for a professional job.
   He's a college graduate, for God's sake! I know he could find a better
   job if he'd try. He acts like he's afraid of a little responsibility!

The list goes on. All of these complaints, and more, are coming from parents who have raised their children to adulthood, but apparently didn't teach and reinforce the previously discussed messages. And the list will continue to lengthen until you wise up, Sister. Who, if not you, is going to make your son or daughter aware of the need to work toward the ultimate goal of becoming a responsible, self-supporting adult? Who, if not you, is going to lovingly guide your children to the realization that this is not only expected, but it is the right thing to do, that to do less serves to create the situations which cause the previously heard complaints, and more!

Sister, complaining about the pressure you feel by having to support and/or subsidize your adult children who, "Talk to me just any kind of way!" does no good. Your adult children who are not in college need to be in their own households. If they are college students, an exception can be made, and justified, because they are in the process of preparing themselves for independency. Conflict is much more likely between you and your adult offspring when he or she is living in your household and being supported by you.

If you are the parent of adult children who have already graduated from college and are working on jobs which require no college degree, and who could probably do better if the appropriate level of effort were extended, don't subsidize them by allowing them to stay in your home and maintain the lifestyle to which you have accustomed them. If you don't enable them, they are more likely to be motivated to get that better job in order to pay their own rent, utilities and car note. While the lower-paying, nonprofessional job that your adult offspring currently holds might pay his car note, car insurance, and buy his gas, it won't stretch to cover his own housing expenses which you are now providing. Don't subsidize him and then complain about the subsidy.

Even if your adult children must hold nonprofessional jobs, and/or must work for minimum wages because they do not have the skills to get professional jobs, they still need to support themselves, at whatever level they are able. This might even motivate them to pursue additional job training!

It is not an easy task for any of us who have raised children from infancy to adulthood to accept that these once helpless newborns are now adults. But it is a fact of life for many of us. Tack on top of this the fact that these once upon a time helpless children are now adults, and expect to be treated as adults by you as well as others. Tack on top of this the fact that you expect to have some authority when your money is doing the supporting. Tack on top of this the fact that your adult children already resent that they are dependent upon Mom and Dad, and then it becomes easy to understand why there is conflict in many homes between parents whose adult children are still living at home. No adult wants to have to borrow the car, as he or she did as a teenager. No adult wants to have to ask for gas money, to be told how long he or she can be gone in the car, etc. These are things that cause resentment to build because they are demeaning to an adult.

Prepare your children to work hard preparing themselves for independency. Set the stage early in their lives. It cannot be stressed too forcefully that the obligation to do so is **yours**. If you fail to do so, don't expect that someone else will, and don't expect that it will just happen. There are many things in life that just happen, but becoming a successful, independent person as an adult is not one of those things. Preparation is required, and preparing your children for success is your responsibility. Why should someone else assume it? If you fail to do it, don't expect that at some magical age your child will be magically transported into self-supporting adulthood, or that your child will magically understand that Mom can no longer be expected to happily foot the bills for his or her expenses. This kind of thinking does not just naturally happen. It becomes a natural part of a child's maturation processes only when it is taught and reinforced as the child grows and develops.

Don't miss the opportunity to point out to your children as you watch a television show or movie with them, what happens when adult children are allowed to reach maturity with no understanding of the need to work to succeed in life Do this so that they look forward to being self-supporting and independent; point out also, the rewards of fulfillment that this brings.

Bottom line: You are obligated to raise your children so that they anticipate becoming mature, self-supporting individuals. Do so, and you will suffer no pang of conscience for having done what is not only the right thing to do, but a life-long, rewarding accomplishment for both you and your children!

Chapter IX

Raising Grandchildren While Your Adult Children Party

Sister, **it's not okay to parent your grandchildren while your own adult children party** (and for the purpose of this discussion, the term, "party," means any activity which enables your adult children to fail to take responsibility for their own child or children). It doesn't matter how good it feels to hold and to pamper that grandchild, or those grandchildren. It doesn't matter what your thoughts are concerning having another chance to do it right, to correct or make amends for some of the errors you made while raising your own child or children. The fact of the matter is, your child is now an adult with a child of her own, and you enable her to fail to assume the role that any responsible adult is obligated to assume: **that of raising his or her own child, or children,** when you step in as a surrogate.

First of all, if God had meant most women who are old enough to be grandmothers to raise children, there would probably be no such thing as menopause. As a God-fearing woman myself, I believe, very firmly, that God's designs are best for His people. God has designed, in most instances, for a woman's childbearing years to be limited. It logically follows that a woman's child-rearing years should also be limited. Now this doesn't mean that those of us who have raised successful children to adulthood should not share and participate to assist younger mothers to do the same, but it does mean that we, in most instances, should not have the seven days a week, twenty-four hours a day responsibility for a child, or children, that we were obligated to assume when our own children were still in the home. This is a formidable task for anybody, and it is certainly one for which most grandparents should not be responsible. When we, God's people, fail to follow his plan, we create gargantuan problems for ourselves. Of course when we take children into our homes, we take them into our hearts, and in a different way from the way we do as grandparents who live in separate quarters. We take them into our hearts as our children, children for whom we feel responsible, yet, as their grandparents, we take the liberty to indulge them, as we would never have done our own children when we were raising them. This creates a situation for you, the grandparent, and for the child, or children, that is a no-win situation.

As an intelligent adult, Sister, you know what happens to children who are overly-indulged. They don't become adequately socialized. And make no mistake about it: all children are born unsocialized. We are responsible for socializing our children. They cannot be allowed to just grow up. Merely having another birthday pass does not guarantee socialization. As a veteran teacher, I speak from very personal experience that this is a truth. Too many times I have had this thought: a child in sixth, seventh, or eighth grade should know better than that. But I've come to the conclusion that I'm wrong. While it is a normal expectation of a teacher of children who are twelve, thirteen, fourteen years old, or older, " that they should know better than that," when I examine my own experiences, I easily see that I am expecting these children to know, without having been taught, what I had to be taught to know: to speak in whispers in certain environments, like the library, for instance; not to speak when someone else is speaking; not to talk back to adults; not to assume a posture of disrespect, even when remaining silent; to respect the school environment and property; to think before I speak; to raise my hand and wait to be recognized before speaking out in class; that it was inappropriate to just blurt out, any time I had a thought; to respect authority.

Our children are not practicing these and other appropriate behaviors because they have not been taught, from a very early age, that they were expected to practice them. We, Sisters, have failed to teach them in our homes. And we cannot expect our mothers and fathers to teach them. It is not our parents' responsibility to socialize our children. A whole different level of socialization is demanded now. When our parents were raising us, all of the negative examples that are part of our children's everyday lives were not factors in ours. We didn't see children on television disrespect adults to provide so-called entertainment for an audience. We didn't see other kids in our classes disrespecting the teacher. There are so many negative influences in our children's lives to which we, as children, were not exposed. And because this is so, many of our parents are unequipped to deal with the socialization of today's child. Today's children must, of necessity, be equipped with socialization skills which will enable them to combat and cope with these negative influences.

Socializing a child in today's society, with its current climate, is an awesome responsibility, and it is one which should not be undertaken, in most instances, by the child's grandparents.

Sisters, we need to reclaim our children. They will continue to practice behaviors which demonstrate that they have not been properly socialized as long as grandparents are doing the raising. Our children need us! Grandparents are wonderful blessings in a child's life, and children who are blessed to know and to interact with their grandparents are indeed fortunate, but it is not the job of a grandparent to parent your child. That job belongs to **you**, Sister!

Our children need to hear, in their homes, on a regular, on-going, basis, and more than once a day, that we will not tolerate any kinds of inappropriate behaviors from them, that we love them too much, and that they are too precious to us to be allowed to engage in uncouth, uncivilized behaviors.

Imagine, if you can, a classroom filled with twenty-five 12 - 15 year old children. Five (or fewer) of these children are all it takes to disrupt the meaningful, educational activities which have been planned for the children. Granted, most of the children will be attentive to the teacher, or at the very least, will feign attentiveness, if there are no class clowns in the room. But for every child who is disruptive and disrespectful, there is at least one other (and sometimes more than one), who will give his attention to, or attempt to mimic, the class clown.

Sister, the previous scenario is a fact of life for thousands of teachers and children every school day. You see, when our children are born to teenaged (and sometimes even preteen) unwed mothers, and are being raised, for the most part, by indulgent grandparents, the results are what we are currently experiencing.

It's not enough for us to expect them to know better. They do know, on some levels, that they should do these things, or that they should not do those things, but it is obvious to those of us who have daily contact with children, that just knowing isn't good enough. Just knowing isn't motivation enough for our children to practice these behaviors on an on-going basis. Our children need to hear, from us, that they are to respect authority, and we need to be the first authority in their lives from whom respect is demanded. We can't be that, Sister, we can't do that, unless we live our lives in such a way that we can, not only command their respect, but demand it. We can't do that unless we live respectably. One clear demonstration of respectable living by adults who have children, is the parenting of their own children.

What our children need to know is that it is important to us that they practice appropriate behaviors consistently. They need to know that our expectations are that they will always be respectful, not only to us, but to their teachers, as well as other adults in their lives, that they will always respect the school environment and property. They need to know that it is not just their right, it is also their privilege, to be able to attend school and to receive an education, free of charge, and that they can repay their obligation for receiving this free education by becoming productive citizens. They need to know that people had to bleed and die so that this privilege would be extended to them, so that this right would become theirs, and that they make a mockery of these people's blood and deaths when they behave as if the privilege is of no consequence. Parents need to articulate these truths to their children, repeatedly, lovingly, firmly, and we need to do so in our homes, so that they become indelibly imprinted upon each child's psyche, and so that each child realizes just how important it is to us that they always practice appropriate behaviors, always! Then, it becomes important to them also.

Our children need to know that not just their teachers, but that their parents consider certain behaviors uncivilized, and that you won't tolerate uncivilized behaviors from your beloved children.

They need to hear this from their parents, long before they become school-aged. They need to hear from you, "Don't do that! Don't say things like that!" Not after they have embarrassed you in the company of others, but when you are alone with them and they do or say something that is inappropriate. They need to know that some behaviors are considered inappropriate. They need a clear definition, from you, of the term, "inappropriate." They need a clear idea of the behaviors that you consider inappropriate.

Sister, do you realize that many of our children really do not know what is inappropriate because they are being raised by grandparents who are not aware that these children have to be told things that we, their children, did not have to be told, things that we understood intuitively, because of the climate during the times in which we were being reared, and we have neglected to teach them ourselves. We have been so busy with "our own lives" that we have neglected the most important people in our lives: **our children.** Oh, we've bought them things, and played with them for a few minutes when they were little kids, but we've neglected them to the point that by the time they enter their teens, we're running from them. I don't mean running in the literal sense (even though some parents are running in the literal sense), but think about it. When was the last time you actually looked forward to spending several hours in the company of your teen? When was the last time one of your friends told you of looking forward to spending a few hours with his or her teen? But I'll bet you don't have to look too distant into the past to recall the following or similar complaints: "She has a smart mouth on her; he's too aggressive; he's smelling himself," etc.

Sister, don't you know that we've allowed our children's behavior to get to the point where we can't stand our own children! When school is not in session, we can hardly wait for it to start back. Have you ever taken the time to analyze why this is so? Do you remember your own teen years? During summers when schools were not in session, if both our parents were required to be away from the home, and they said to us, "Stay in the house until we get home, or stay in the backyard," there was no question that we obeyed. Our parents didn't "run" from us. If there was any fleeing done, we did it! The reason: We had been taught respect and obedience from our earliest existence. We had seen our older siblings behave with respect and obedience. There was no consideration, nor expectation, of any other behavior. We had been taught these behaviors by our parents, not by indulgent grandparents who were, and still are, already tired from all of the years they spent rearing their own children!

Grandmothers, don't enable and encourage your daughters to have other children, illegitimate or otherwise, that they are not in a position to nurture and care for. Every intelligent woman knows that motherhood should also mean parenting. Your daughters should have the joy and the pain associated with parenting their own children. Do not enable them to relinquish this responsibility and miss out on the pain, the joy, or the fulfillment it can bring! It is through parenting that bonding occurs, and this bonding must take place during the early months and years of a child's life. When you intervene, Grandmother, however willing and thankful your daughter may be for this intervention, no matter how willing you are, you rob your daughter and her child of the bonding process that, in all likelyhood, can and will occur, if you do not intervene. Grandmother, you do have a responsibility here, but it is not one of parenting your grandchildren. Your responsibility is to help your daughter to understand that her children are her responsibility and that she should do the parenting.

Do not wait until your daughter has a baby to teach her this important lesson: you are responsible for any child to whom you give birth. If you're wise, you'll wait until you are well-educated, and married, before becoming a mother. If, and when, this lesson is taught and instilled throughout a girl's formative years, it becomes indelibly seared within her psyche, and she is not likely to violate herself with an illegitimate child. When she does decide to have a child, she will be educated as well as married, and she will look forward, joyfully, to parenting her own child. If this is what you want for your daughter, don't enable her to do the opposite easily. Sometimes tough love is the only kind of love that is effective!

Enough said! However, there is one other thing that demands mention in this chapter. Grandmother, if you are married, don't neglect your husband and behave as though his feelings are unimportant. More likely than not, he will not be at all agreeable to disrupting his life to raise another child, even a beloved grandchild. Hear him. A grandchild, in most cases, should not be raised by grandparents. When he or she is, the **grand** diminishes or disappears altogether, and all that remains is "parent" only.

Chapter X

Making Welfare a Way of Life

Sister, **it is wrong to make welfare a way of life**, to have every intention of being dependent upon the government for your daily needs for the rest of your life. It is wrong to feel that because you made the choice to have children, someone else owes you for their care and upkeep. While it is a fact of life that children need care and upkeep, it is also a fact of life that all of us are aware that this is so, long before we make the decision to have a child.

You, and you alone, are responsible for assuring that you don't have to depend upon the government to feed and clothe your children. Even though we all know that our children's fathers should also contribute to assuring this, we are also aware that this might not be so, which is why it is so important for us to prepare ourselves before we have children so that we are in a position to care for them, financially, if we have to do so.

To depend on the government for one's subsistence is demeaning, it does not inspire confidence, it is not a good example to set for our children, it lowers one's self-esteem, it limits where one can live; it limits one's aspirations. Dependency on welfare shrinks a person's world; it does the opposite of expand one's horizons. It places you and your children in an environment where friendships and attachments are formed with others who have all of the above limitations. This means that your child, or children, may be twice as likely to find themselves involved in the criminal justice system as people whose circumstances differ drastically.

Sister, do you realize that some of us can trace welfare involvement in our lives, in our homes, as far back as our memories will allow? That's sad, Sister; that's wrong. And while we are not, and certainly cannot be held responsible for being children on the welfare rolls, we alone can assure that our own children are never enrolled, and that our children's children do not become welfare brats, to which children whose parents are on welfare are sometimes referred.

"Now how am I supposed to do that?" you cry. First of all, set the example. If you were a child on the welfare rolls, I'll wager you often wished that your parents could support you like Don, or Mary, or Sue's parents did them. I'll bet there were times when you promised yourself that you'd not allow that to happen to your kids. Yet, it has happened. Let's pause for a minute and examine why.

Know this: children learn what they live, and they live what they are allowed to experience. This is the main reason why so many of us do so many things as adults, just as our parents did them when we were children, in spite of the fact that we promised ourselves, passionately, I'll never do this or that as Mama did! And in all likelyhood, your children are going to do just as you did, no matter what passionate promises they make to themselves about doing the contrary. This is a primary reason why we, as parents, are obligated to set examples for our children that we want to see them emulate.

Our children know almost nothing when they are born, but they are capable of learning almost anything! They are going to learn what we teach them, whether we set out to teach them something intentionally, or whether we model the behavior and teach them by example.

When a family has been on welfare for several generations, a number of actions occur, almost subliminally. Consider the following: Jennie was born in 1975 to an unwed, teen mother in the 9th grade. Jennie lived with her mother, Jean, and her grandmother, Jerri. The three of them lived in a subsidized housing complex in a large, eastern city. Jennie's mother, Jean, was barely fifteen when she gave birth, and was unmarried. Jean's mother, Jerri had been an unwed, teen mother when her daughter, Jean had been born. Both Jean and Jerri have been receiving welfare checks for the past thirty years (if you combine the years each of them has been on welfare), and they both had hoped that Jennie would stay in school, graduate, get a good job, and break the welfare cycle in her life.

They were disappointed when Jennie confessed that she was two months pregnant and had just missed her third menstrual cycle, but not greatly surprised. After all, Jennie was in the 11th grade by this time, so she had stayed in school longer than both her mother and grandmother. Jennie was disappointed in herself, but this was a behavior pattern that Jennie had internalized, and so she couldn't help but feel familiar with this pattern. She was surrounded by other girls whose circumstances were identical to her own, and many who were already unwed, teen mothers.

When Jennie gave birth to twin boys, prematurely, the boys required incubation and extended hospitalization. Neither Jennie, Jean, or Jerri had expected twins, premature births, nor the need for extended hospitalization for the newborns. They had no medical insurance; they had no savings. Welfare to the rescue!

Jennie was depressed for weeks following the births. She hadn't even wanted one child, but now she had two, and no means to care for them, except by adding them to the welfare rolls.

The twins, whom Jennie named Kerry and Jerry, had been in the hospital for three weeks when they were taken out of the incubators; another two weeks when they were scheduled to be released. During these two weeks, Jennie had been thinking long and hard about caring for two babies, boys no less, about whom she knew very little. She had been thinking about providing for their needs, long term. Without saying anything to Jean and Jerri, Jennie had decided to give the twins up for adoption. She had listened to all kinds of advice about this possibility, so she knew that there were several childless couples who would love to have the twins.

Because she didn't want either of them trying to change her mind, she was vague whenever Jerri or Jean asked her about the twin's release date. She didn't even ask either of them to ride the bus with her to the hospital. Her best friend, in whom she had confided, drove her there. She signed papers agreeing to the twin's adoption. She returned home hours later that day just as if she had been to the hospital for a visit with the twins. This continued for the better part of the following week, then Jennie lowered the boom. She confessed to her mother and grandmother that the twins were now with their new family. Needless to say, they were at first disbelieving, later tearful and accusatory.

"I can't believe you'd give your own blood away like that!" Jean shouted. "You knew we'd take care of those kids!"

"With what, Mama? How many times have I heard you say, money doesn't grow on trees?" How many times have you told me that I need a part-time job because your welfare check barely covers our living expenses, that there's nothing left over for extras? Did you tell me, just before I found out that I was pregnant, that if I wanted to go with my class on the junior class trip, I'd better find a way to make some extra money? So tell me, how were you going to help me take care of them?" Jennie asks quietly.

"We would've managed somehow! You know we would have!" Jerri put in.

"We probably would have, Gran, but 'somehow' isn't good enough. The three of us are managing 'somehow' right now, and we're living witnesses that 'somehow' isn't good enough. People are out there living, and I mean really living, not just existing from welfare check to welfare check, or selling drugs! People are out there going on vacations, buying cars and driving to supermarkets instead of walking to neighborhood grocery stores where everything costs twice as much, and buying boats, and big screen televisions. A lot of my classmates are already applying to colleges. I want all of that for myself. I want all of that for Kerry and Jerry, and since I can't provide any of those things for them, I've given them to people who can. They'll have both a mom and a dad to take care of them, to plan for them, and to love them. They deserve that," Jennie concludes.

"You never said anything to me before about a father. I told you years ago that he was just a boy whose family moved here from somewhere down south. We dated for a while, his family didn't like it here, so they moved back south, and then I discovered that I was pregnant with you. I've never missed him, and you never gave any indication that you did either," Jean tells Jennie.

"Mom, how can I miss someone I never even met? I didn't miss him, not in the way you mean. But I have wondered what he looked like, if I looked like him, since I don't look like you do. And I do wonder if he would have wanted me if he had known about me. And remember that time when I was in 7th grade and my softball team sponsored that father/daughter banquet? Well, I just pretended to be sick that day at school so nobody would expect me to be at the banquet that night. I knew I didn't have a dad to bring me. I'm not going to do that to my kids. When school starts back, I'm going back to school, and I'm going to graduate. And I'm going to find a way to go to college. You said earlier that you would've helped me with the twins. Well, you can still help me. Help me go back to school. Help me to stay in school. Help me to go to college. Will you still help me?" Jennie asks.

All three of them, Jerri, not yet fifty; Jean, only thirty-one, and Jennie, sixteen, cried, and hugged and kissed. Jennie vowed, silently, to break the welfare cycle in her family. She didn't confide this to Jean or Jerri. She knew they'd enough to handle for that day. But she promised herself to find out more about that nursing assistant program that her friend's aunt had recently completed. Maybe she could get her mother and grandmother interested in getting that training and eventually breaking the welfare cycle in their lives. Both of them are younger than Pam's Aunt Rena is, she says to herself.

Won't you do the same for yourself and your family? No matter how many generations of your family have been bound to the welfare system, the welfare cycle can be broken, the shackles of welfare can be loosed, but only by those who have allowed the system to enslave them. Pledge to loosen those shackles. Free yourself and your children. You deserve better! Your children deserve better! The decision is yours. What choice will you make?

Epilogue

Sisters, as one popular comedienne is known for saying, "Let's talk." Let's talk about how often we feel disrespected. Let's talk about how frequently we are heard to complain and/or listen to the complaints of other sisters about being disrespected. Let's talk about being "dogged" by boyfriends, men, lovers, even husbands.   Let's examine why this is such a reiterative occurrence in our lives.

How many of us have given birth to children while we were still single women? How many of us have allowed men to come into our homes, which we share with our children, and spend the night in our beds, with our children right there in the home? How many of us have allowed men to move into the homes which we share with our children without benefit of clergy? How many of us have left our children alone at home, for days at a time, to spend time with some man? How many of us have dated, and deliberately allowed another woman's husband to impregnate us with the sole intention of "getting him," and yet didn't? Do you still wonder why?

Sisters, all of us learned, a long time ago, the difference between right and wrong. Most of us learned, a long time ago, the difference between appropriate and inappropriate. All of us know the difference between good and bad. All of us know when we are doing something we want our children to emulate, as opposed to when we are doing something we hope they'll never repeat, or even know about.

Our mothers and grandmothers, many of whom have passed on, would "turn over in their graves," if they were privy to some of the activities in which we have engaged, in spite of their love for us, their sacrifices for us; in spite of their instructions to us, and in spite of the Christian legacy many of them left to us. Some of our mothers and grandmothers who are still alive today are trying to figure out where they went wrong. Many of them know they taught us better than that. Many of them know they set the right examples for us. They have no idea why we behave as if the term "morals" is something to be feared, something to be spurned!

Sisters, plain and simple: if we want to be respected, we're going to have to behave respectably. Nobody respects a woman who murders her children. "Isn't that a little drastic?" you ask. Think about it. Some our children are dying in gang related warfare; they're dying in drive-by shootings; they're dying in street fights; they're dying drug-related deaths. Others are living, but their hopes are dead. Their dads are nonentities in their lives; they rarely see their mothers because they have been dumped off on grandmothers; they're dying inside, and many of us are oblivious to their pain. Many of us are so busy "living our lives" that we are keeping our children from living theirs. In a sense we're killing our children! You see, the lives of our children should be filled with wholesome learning experiences.

Sisters, Zora Neale Hurston said over a half century ago, "I can make something out of the children. They have the essence of greatness in them."

Today, that essence of greatness is still visible in the children, and I beseech you to enable them to realize this greatness. Please, nurture the children. Please, please, empower them to come to school without troubled minds. Nurture our sons so that invisible chips never perch on their shoulders. Nurture our daughters so that they are capacitated to move from childhood through puberty into young womanhood with a clear mental image of their real self-worth. I implore you to nurture the children. There is the essence of greatness in them!

Our children's lives should be filled daily with parental contact of a pleasant nature, involving teaching, learning, loving, and bonding. But these experiences are nonexistent in many of our children's lives. Many of them never sit down around the dinner table in their homes with their parents and siblings for a home-cooked meal. Don't you realize, Sisters, that this is when table manners are taught? Is there any wonder why so many of our children demonstrate that they have none when they eat in their schools' cafeterias? Sandwiches and cereal constitute the bulk of their diets. And while there is nothing wrong with either of these, our children deserve, and need, more from us. They need what our parents gave us, **and more.** They need fully functional families comprised of healthy mothers and fathers. And many of them have never had, and will never have that. And adults have the nerve to wonder, out loud, why children are so different now from how we were when we were children!

I know, you're thinking: what can I do about the fact that his father wants no part of the family? Sister, put your focus on what you can do; forget about what you can't do. You can give your children a positive, functional, respectable mother. You can see that your children have well-balanced meals. You can see that your family sits down around the dinner table, on a regular basis, to eat a home-cooked meal. You can show up for P.T.A. Meetings, once a month, at your children's schools. You can take an active interest in your children's school and homework assignments. You can show up for parent conferences to discuss your children's progress, or lack thereof; don't wait until you are forced to show up in order to get your child reinstated in school following a suspension. When you do all of the things that you can do for your children, the deficiencies in your children's lives begin to minimize. There is so much that you can do to provide a healthy environment in which your children can move toward the maturation process that, if you do those things, your children will, in all probability, do fine as children, and mature into healthy, functional adults.

Finally, Sisters, we all realize that we have received more than our fair share of disrespect. And we probably will always be disrespected by someone at sometime, if for no other reason than the fact that we are females. But keep this in mind: the **disrespect does not have to be self-inflicted.** We can say no, I just will not do that, whenever we are asked to engage in any of the **Top Ten** behaviors discussed in this book.

Sisters, our children need us. And you're absolutely right when you say, "I can't make their father stay here if he doesn't want to stay." But what you can do is be there yourself for your children. You can set the right examples for your children to emulate.

Sisters, if you already have children who were born to you while you were still single women, only you can make sure that any other children born to you will be born under the right circumstances. Young Sister, if you have no children yet, make sure that any children born to you are born under the right circumstances.   You know, right now, what the right circumstances are. This is one decision over which you have total control.   Pledge to become or to remain celibate, if you are single. Pledge to get saved, by God's grace, if you are unsaved, and He'll empower you. And when a Christian brother comes along who wants you, he will marry you! He'll marry you, if it is God's will, because he'll respect you enough to know that you'll settle for no less. He'll respect you enough to know that he should offer you no less because to do so would be to disrespect you, and he will not be in a position to justify doing that! And if God does not will it, He will help you to realize that you are better off without that brother! In the words of Spike Lee, "Do the right thing." You will never feel remorse for having done so!

Note to Reader

A final note, Sisters, to you. As I have traveled and lived throughout this country, I have been privileged to teach thousands of children during my career. Many of you have beautiful, intelligent, intuitive, and articulate children, many of whom have managed to excel, in part, because of the positive influences you have been in their lives, in spite of your pain and suffering; in spite of the fact that you have had to raise them alone with no fathers in the homes, and for so doing, you deserve the applause of all sisters, **everywhere!** Know that you have mine! Some of the children have been successful in school in spite of the disillusionments which they have been forced to tolerate in their short lifetimes. This "Essence of greatness" referred to by Zora Neale Hurston over a half century ago, I have been privileged to glimpse during my numerous interactions with children.

Many of your children have unburdened their souls in my presence, crying out their anguish, reaching out to someone for comfort who cares. I have heard their cries of pain; I have seen their grimaces of discomfort. I have counseled with children whose mothers are hooked on drugs, and whose fathers they have

never even met. I have counseled with children whose brothers
and/or fathers are in jail, and who, because they love their
brothers and fathers, must take the position that, "There is
nothing wrong with going to jail!" I have worked with children
whose mothers were in rehab, and these children were virtually
homeless, or were in homes where they knew they were
unwelcome intruders! Imagine, if you can, being a powerless
child in that position! I have done what I could to comfort, and I
pray that I have helped to ease their discomfort, but nobody can
comfort a child like "Mother," like "Dad," because these are the
people to whom children should be able, as well as willing, to
reach out for comfort. Instead, however, all too frequently,
these are the people who are causing the pain and discomfort in
the lives of children.

I have seen countless children "act out" because of their pain
and discomfort, unable, as well as unwilling, to share their
reasons for these inappropriate expressions. When asked, "What
is the matter?" their response is almost always, "Nothing!" But
the common thread, whether in Philadelphia where I worked at a
school for boys only, between the ages of thirteen through
nineteen, who had been committed there by the courts, or in Geor-
gia, where I initially worked with children in the fifth grade whom
I thought of as mere babies when I first started the job, but was to

was to learn that they were savvy about things to which they should have not been privy, this common thread was every child's desire to be comforted by "Mom" and "Dad." The common thread has been, and I believe will always be, the desire of children to have cohesive parents who plan for them, who interact lovingly with them as well as with one another, and who are concerned for their safety and their success, parents who obviously love them and will accept only the best for them and from them because of their love. You see, children don't care about our emotions. We can lament to anyone who will listen to us about how much we love our children, but this lamentation is meaningless to a child unless we translate it into action. Again, children do not care about our emotions, but they care a great deal about the behavior generated as a result of our emotions! Think about all of the talk shows you've watched where brothers tell the world that they love their children, but left them when they were helpless babies. Who is to say? It is not for any of us to judge what is in another man's heart. Perhaps these men do feel that they love their children, but like the children, we could care less for the emotions they experience when their behavior dictates the exact opposite of what their mouths express.

I wish many of you could observe your children when they are in the classroom and have just grasped a new concept, or generated a noteworthy idea. Their eyes glow beautifully, their enthusiasm is magnetic, their hands go up, as if they are about to burst forth and fly, and for a little while, it is obvious that they have been able to forget about the problems which have become central to their very existence. For a brief time, they are able to function as "regular" children whose only problems are kid-related ones. I wish you could observe them in the classroom when they cause disruptions to the educational setting, refuse to comply with established rules and regulations, and then respond in inappropriate ways when confronted.

Would that you could get into their minds, and through some osmotic process, get a clear picture of how having to deal with adult-generated problems, impact them. Perhaps then you would be motivated to seek to create for them what they deserve: **a period in their lives when they can be children, a period when they can grow, and learn, and be happy.** A period when they don't have to be concerned about where their next meal is coming from; a period when they can rest easy, and not worry about some strange man in their homes causing them discomfort; a period when their school clothes are washed, and pressed, and matched for them, and laid out before they arise for school, on a daily basis! A period when a hot breakfast, a hug, and a kiss await them before they leave for school each day; a period when they know that at least one loving parent joyfully anticipates their return from school each day.

These are amenities to which every child is entitled, and deserving, yet they are amenities that so few of our children are able to take for granted, as so many of us did when we were children.

Sisters, you need to know that our children are impacted, in a negative way or in a positive way, by whether or not they are privileged to enjoy these amenities. And I speak from very personal experience when I tell you that it becomes obvious to those of us who work with children in the school systems throughout this country, which children are the ones who are able to take these amenities for granted. These are the children who are outgoing, cooperative, happy, well-liked; these are the children who get along well with their teachers as well as their peers. These are the children who don't walk around with invisible chips on their shoulders. These are the children who recognize that their grades are earned, not given to them, and they can accept the grades which they have earned without feeling undue animosity for their teachers. They can decide within themselves that "I'm going to improve this grade, or these grades for the next grading period." They are able to do so because they have not lived with the guilt of blame all of their young lives. They have not blamed themselves for the fact that their dads have always been nonentities in their lives, or have left their homes. They have not felt the lash of blame emanating from their mothers' whips because they resemble their unfaithful fathers. And so, they have no preconception that blame means that there is something intrinsically wrong with them.

The female children in the latter category are the girls who value themselves because they have always been valued by their parents, and consequently, they know that they have value. They are not interested in becoming responsible for another life before they are empowered and enabled to become responsible for themselves. These are the girls who will not violate themselves with illegitimate babies, who are no less precious, but definitely less advantaged.   And here I do not necessarily mean disadvantaged in the economic sense, though this is also usually true for many of them. Here I mean disadvantaged in the sense that they are not born to married, cohesive parents who joyfully anticipate their births. These are the girls who know that happy families and happy marriages do exist outside of fairy tales because they, themselves, are witnesses to their parents' happy marriages, and are members of happy families.

The boys who are privileged to be born to cohesive, married couples are the ones who do not walk around with invisible chips on their shoulders, angry at the world, blaming all the men they encounter for their anger, their problems. The ones for whom the opposite is true are those who do have these chips on their shoulders, the ones who do blame all men for the blame they would like to express to their fathers who are not involved in their lives. These are the boys who also show disrespect to females because the one female central to their very existence has shown herself unworthy of respect, and so the boy takes the position, usually subconsciously initially, that I can't respect my mother, so no female will get any respect from me!

The privileged boys are the ones who are able to make the journey through adolescence without ending up involved in the juvenile, criminal justice system. This is so because it is a rare boy who will not listen, and take the advice to heart, from a loving, committed parent for whom he has always had respect, and to whom he has always gone for advice and comfort throughout his formative years.

Sister, your child is a rare and beautiful gift, given to you by God, for a temporary time period. You can mold him or her, and you will mold your child, whether intentionally, or unintentionally. This being a fact, think very seriously about your own behavior. Realize the potential repercussions your behavior can, and probably will, have upon how your child turns out in life.

You will impact your child's thought processes, and your child's thought processes will dictate his or her behavior! Be cognizant of how powerfully you have been impacted by your own parents' actions. Use your adroitness to impact your child to advantage, yours as well as his or hers.

Finally, know this: One day your child will be mature enough to realize that you lead him or her down the right path, or that you lead him or her down the path to destruction: prison, drugs, prostitution, gang affiliation, etc.; or one day your child will fathom that he or she had a really good mother, who did not allow him or her to do those things which were potentially self-destructive.

For the sake of the children, let us express, not just with our mouths, but with our actions, that we do love them, that we want only the best for them, and that we will accept nothing less than the best from them. Let us remove **"I can't"** from our vocabularies when it comes to our children's lives, and well-being, and let's get on about the business of setting the kinds of examples that will make a concrete reality of these positive expectations!

_____

Your Name

My Top Ten List

Use this page for your own **Top Ten List** of things which are not okay.

1. _____

2. _____

3. _____

4. _____

5. _____

6. _____

7. _____

8. _____

9. _____

10. _____

Share your Top Ten with another Sister. Together we will triumph!

I TOO HAVE A DREAM

Joyce Willard Teal

Like the Dr. Martin Luther King,
As a teacher, I too have a dream.
I dream of a world where children are free
To grow, and to learn, and to be somebody.

I too have a dream where children are planned;
Not created on the mere whim of a man.
I dream of a world where children are raised,
Where their mistakes are tolerated, and their accomplishments
praised.

I, too, have a dream of schools that are fun
Because learning is given priority by everyone!
Education is the target and the results at the end!
Children accept teachers and parents as their very best friends.

I dream of a world where children feel that they belong,
Where the two people who produce them also make for them a
home!
In this dream that I have, all children are cherished;
None are deserted, neglected, or left alone to perish!

This is one dream from which I'm not anxious to awaken.
In this dream, no child is forsaken.
Every child is entitled to, and enjoys childhood;
Every child has his needs met and his problems understood!

This is one dream that I wish were reality.
This is one dream that our world needs so desperately!
Too many of our children are suffering and in pain,
But in my dream, love and security reign!